ISBN 978-0-364-64244-3
PIBN 11274226

This book is a reproduction of an important historical work. Forgotten Books uses
state-of-the-art technology to digitally reconstruct the work, preserving the original format
whilst repairing imperfections present in the aged copy. In rare cases, an imperfection in
the original, such as a blemish or missing page, may be replicated in our edition. We do,
however, repair the vast majority of imperfections successfully; any imperfections that
remain are intentionally left to preserve the state of such historical works.

1 MONTH OF
FREE
READING

at
www.ForgottenBooks.com

By purchasing this book you are eligible for one month membership to ForgottenBooks.com, giving you unlimited access to our entire collection of over 1,000,000 titles via our web site and mobile apps.

To claim your free month visit:
www.forgottenbooks.com/free1274226

English
Français
Deutsche
Italiano
Español
Português

www.forgottenbooks.com

Mythology Photography **Fiction**
Fishing Christianity **Art** Cooking
Essays Buddhism Freemasonry
Medicine **Biology** Music **Ancient
Egypt** Evolution Carpentry Physics
Dance Geology **Mathematics** Fitness
Shakespeare **Folklore** Yoga Marketing
Confidence Immortality Biographies
Poetry **Psychology** Witchcraft
Electronics Chemistry History **Law**
Accounting **Philosophy** Anthropology
Alchemy Drama Quantum Mechanics
Atheism Sexual Health **Ancient History**
Entrepreneurship Languages Sport
Paleontology Needlework Islam
Metaphysics Investment Archaeology
Parenting Statistics Criminology
Motivational

liographic Notes / Notes technique et bibliographiques

the best original
this copy which
may alter any of
or which may
od of filming are

L'Institut a microfilmé le meilleur examplaire qu'il lui a
été possible de se procurer. Les détails de cet exemplaire qui sont peut-être uniques du point de vue bibli-
ographique, qui peuvent modifier une image reproduite,
ou qui peuvent exiger une modifications dans la méthode normale de filmage sont indiqués ci-dessous.

☐ Coloured pages / Pages de couleur

☐ Pages damaged / Pages endommagées

☐ Pages restored and/or laminated /
Pages restaurées et/ou pelliculées

☑ Pages discoloured, stained or foxed /
Pages décolorées, tachetées ou piquées

ture manque

es en couleur

☐ Pages detached / Pages détachées

lack) /
ou noire)

☑ Showthrough / Transparence

☐ Quality of print varies /
Qualité inégale de l'impression

☐ Includes supplementary material /
Comprend du matériel supplémentaire

☐ Pages wholly or partially obscured by errata
slips, tissues, etc., have been refilmed to
ensure the best possible image / Les pages
totalement ou partiellement obscurcies par un
feuillet d'errata, une pelure, etc., ont été filmées

or distortion
serrée peut
n le long de

à nouveau de façon à obtenir la meilleure
image possible.

may appear
these have
ue certaines
restauration
cela était

☐ Opposing pages with varying colouration or
discolourations are filmed twice to ensure the
best possible image / Les pages s'opposant
ayant des colorations variables ou des décol-
orations sont filmées deux fois afin d'obtenir la
meilleur image possible.

L'exemplaire filmé fut reproduit grâce à la
générosité de:

Bibliothèque nationale du Canada

Les images suivantes ont été reproduites avec le
plus grand soin, compte tenu de la condition et
de la netteté de l'exemplaire filmé, et en
conformité avec les conditions du contrat de
filmage.

Les exemplaires originaux dont la couverture en
papier est imprimée sont filmés en commençant
par le premier plat et en terminant soit par la
dernière page qui comporte une empreinte
d'impression ou d'illustration, soit par le second
plat, selon le cas. Tous les autres exemplaires
originaux sont filmés en commençant par la
première page qui comporte une empreinte
d'impression ou d'illustration et en terminant par
la dernière page qui comporte une telle
empreinte.

Un des symboles suivants apparaîtra sur la
dernière image de chaque microfiche, selon le
cas: le symbole ⟶ signifie "A SUIVRE", le
symbole ▼ signifie "FIN".

Les cartes, planches, tableaux, etc., peuvent être
filmés à des taux de réduction différents.
Lorsque le document est trop grand pour être
reproduit en un seul cliché, il est filmé à partir
de l'angle supérieur gauche, de gauche à droite,
et de haut en bas, en prenant le nombre
d'images nécessaire. Les diagrammes suivants
illustrent la méthode.

1

2

3

(ANSI and ISO TEST CHART No. 2)

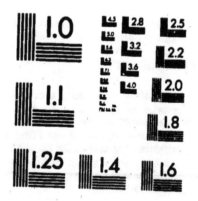

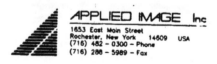

APPLIED IMAGE Inc

1653 East Main Street
Rochester, New York   14609   USA
(716) 482 - 0300 - Phone
(716) 288 - 5989 - Fax

GRAND TRUNK RAILWAY SYSTEM

TOURIST SLEEPING CARS Between

THE EAST AND WEST

CHICAGO & PRINCIPAL POINTS IN THE WESTERN STATES CALIFORNIA & PACIFIC COAST

OCTOBER, 1913

TRAVEL IN A TOURIST CAR

Via the Grand Trunk Railway System — the Double
Track Route Through Canada

TOURIST EXCURSIONS

To Chicago and Principal Points in the Western States,
California and the Pacific Coast

For some years Tourist Sleeping Cars have been operated on fast
express trains, both eastbound and westbound, over the Grand Trunk
Railway System, for the accommodation of passengers who prefer
plain, homelike comforts, instead of the luxurious surroundings of
the modern Pullman Sleeping Cars, such as expensive woodwork and
elaborate upholstering, but both alike are attached to the fast
through express, are operated by the Pullman Company, in charge of

Standard Passenger Train.
Grand Trunk Railway System.

Pullman conductors and porters, and in certain cases of our own
special conductors (who are familiar with all points of interest along
the route), and are well equipped with linen, blankets and mattresses.

While run for the accommodation of holders of second-class tickets
these sleeping cars are equally available for passengers holding first-
class tickets. By their use the cost of the trip is lessened without
sacrifice of any essential comfort. They are neatly furnished, com-
fortably heated, clean and attractive. "Almost as nice as the standard
Pullmans," fairly expresses a comparison between the two styles.

THE TOURIST CAR'S DISTINCTIVE FEATURES

Each of the sections contains an upper and lower berth. By
day the upper is closed, the lower being converted into seats. At
night, when the berths are made up, every section is enclosed on two

1

sides by movable partitions and a curtain in front, affording absolute privacy. The seats are upholstered in black leather with comfortable cushions. There are hooks for hats and wraps. and small detachable folding tables for writing and luncheons. Windows. are double, thereby excluding dust, cinders and draughts. Each window has a movable heavy cloth full length screen, while the aisles are thickly carpeted. The cars are electric lighted, the lights being distributed

Au Revoir.

in the depth by seven sets of three incandescent bulbs each, and there are two electric fans. An enclosed smoking room provides comfortable accommodation for four passengers and is fitted with two metal wash basins with air pressure. water supply. In the ladies' end of the car there are two wash rooms, one on either side of the aisle, with doors with patent catches. Each contains one metal wash basin and commode. All toilet rooms have plate glass mirrors, iced drinking water, soap, towels, combs, brushes. etc. The bedding consists of linen, blankets, pillows and hair mattresses. These tourist cars have steel underframes and wide vestibules, high-back seats, and an oval stained glass above each window.. They are thoroughly cleaned by compressed air and their general appearance both inside and out is attractive in the extreme.

PERSONALLY CONDUCTED EXCURSIONS

A special Grand Trunk conductor travels in the Tourist Car attached to trains on Mondays, Wednesdays and Fridays, from Bosto . to Montreal and from Montreal to Chicago to give assistance and general information as to route traveled, and connections — this Official being in addition to the regular train conductor. Similar service is also afforded on the eastbound trip. leaving Chicago Wednesday, Thursday and Saturday of each week.

From Boston — The Tourist Cars operated over the Grand Trunk Railway System, westbound, leave Boston three times a week, Mondays, Wednesdays and Fridays at 11.05 A.M., running via Boston & Maine Railroad, Central Vermont Railway and Grand Trunk, arriving Chicago 9.25 P.M., Tuesdays, Thursdays and Saturdays. For through time table, see pages 16 and 17.

From **Montreal** — Tourist cars operated over the Grand Trunk Railway System, westbound, leave Montreal three times a week, Mondays, Wednesdays and Fridays, at 10.30 P.M., connecting with the train from Boston arriving at Chicago the following day at 9.25 P.M.

SPECIAL INFORMATION FOR PASSENGERS ARRIVING EX ATLANTIC STEAMERS FROM EUROPE

Second-class tickets are issued in Europe only on the definite understanding that holders desire to avail themselves of the privileges of traveling in the "Tourist Sleeping Car" attached to train, leaving Montreal and Boston for Chicago every Monday, Wednesday and Friday, on payment of an additional charge for sleeping accommodation. (See page 15 for rates for berths.)

Second-class tickets are good on the regular trains or on the "Special" train, meeting the arrival of Atlantic steamers at Quebec, Halifax or Portland, provided train is equipped with second-class cars, otherwise, if holders desire to travel to Montreal by the "Special," in preference to waiting over for the regular train, they have

Comfort in a Tourist Car.

the option of doing so, being accommodated without extra charge in the cars provided for the immigrant or colonist traffic to Western Canada, or in the first-class car (if same is attached to train) on payment of the difference between the local second-class fare and the first-class fare to Montreal, where connection is made with the Tourist Car running on one of the specified days.

By special arrangement sufficiently in advance, "Tourist Sleeping Cars" for all Western points will be attached to the "Special" train on arrival of Atlantic Steamers at Quebec, Halifax or Portland. Passengers holding first-class rail tickets (as well as holders of second-class rail tickets) have the privilege of traveling in the "Tourist Sleeping Car" on payment of an additional charge. (See page 15 for rates for berths).

Electric Locomotive emerging from the St. Clair Tunnel.

Holders of colonist or immigrant tickets may also avail themselves of the privilege of using Tourist Sleeping Cars by paying the difference between the fare they have paid for their tickets and second-class fares plus the regular Tourist Car charges.

BERTH CHARGES

A berth in the Pullman Tourist Car costs much less (about one-half) than in a Standard Sleeping Car. Each berth accommodates two persons without extra sleeper charge; but passengers desiring exclusive use of a berth can obtain it for the price named. (See table of berth rates on page 15).

RESERVATIONS

Reservations for space may be secured by applying to any agent of the Grand Trunk Railway System, giving name of the person or persons for whom accommodation is required, the number of adults, whether married or single, the number of children, age and sex, the point at which car is to be taken and the destination.

MEALS

On the trains on which the Tourist Cars are run, Dining Cars are attached during the day, serving meals and refreshments a la carte.

Those who desire may, of course, carry along lunch baskets with drop handles so that they can be put under the seat when not in use.

BAGGAGE

On each full ticket 150 pounds of baggage will be checked free, and 75 pounds on each half ticket.

Exception.— To points in Manitoba, Saskatchewan and Alberta, 300 pounds of baggage is allowed free for each adult and 150 pounds for each child, to holders of second-class tickets. Excess baggage will be charged for at a low rate per 100 pounds. No piece of baggage weighing over 250 pounds will be accepted.

CHILDREN

No half fare sleeper tickets are sold. Two children between the ages of five and twelve will be considered as one adult. A single child, or infant, accompanied by parent or guardian, will be accommodated in a sleeping berth occupied by the parent or guardian, without charge. The child, however, if between the ages of five and twelve, must hold half fare rail ticket for transportation.

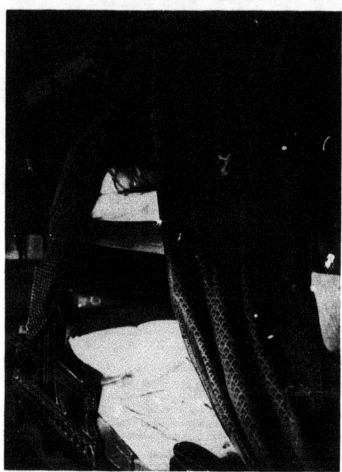

Berths ready to be occupied.

From Boston to Chicago via the Grand Trunk route, the scenery is of a diversified nature and many places of interest and of importance as historical points are seen. Leaving Boston, the important manufacturing cities of Lowell, Worcester, Nashua, Manchester and Concord are passed, and we reach the Central Vermont Railway at White River Junction and proceed through some charming pastoral scenes, passing through the beautiful Green Hills of Vermont with Camel's Hump and Mt. Mansfield, two of Vermont's highest mountains, in view for many miles, until the city of Montreal is reached. Before arriving at the Metropolitan City of the Dominion of Canada, however, one of the most beautiful sights that it is one's good fortune to see is a panoramic view of the city of Montreal as seen from the train while crossing the Victoria Jubilee Bridge (nearly two miles long) over the St. Lawrence River. The scene is one of superb grandeur.

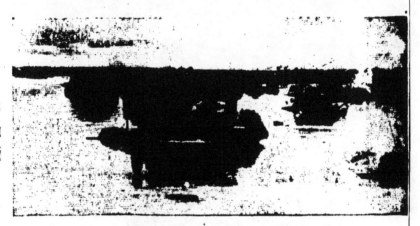

Among the Thousand Islands of the St. Lawrence.

The harbor front of six miles is ablaze with electric lights, and the myriads of twinkling lights along the wharves and covering the city gives one the impression of a city illuminated for some great fete. In the background loom the impressive heights of Mount Royal, from which the city and the island on which it stands was named, while the majestic river twinkles with the lights of its multitude of water craft, large and small. If the passenger reaches Montreal by day the great shipping interests that are centered here are seen and the busy scenes in the harbor are an attractive sight.

From Montreal the route lies westward through some of the principal cities and towns in Canada, and for a distance of nearly eighty miles between Brighton and Toronto vistas of that vast sheet of fresh water, Lake Ontario, are seen from the left of the train. The daylight run from Toronto to London is one of more than usual interest, passing through a fine fruit and agricultural country and proceeding by way of the city of Hamilton. After leaving this city the railway runs along the side of a mountain at the foot of which lies the Dundas Valley, making the view from the train a panorama

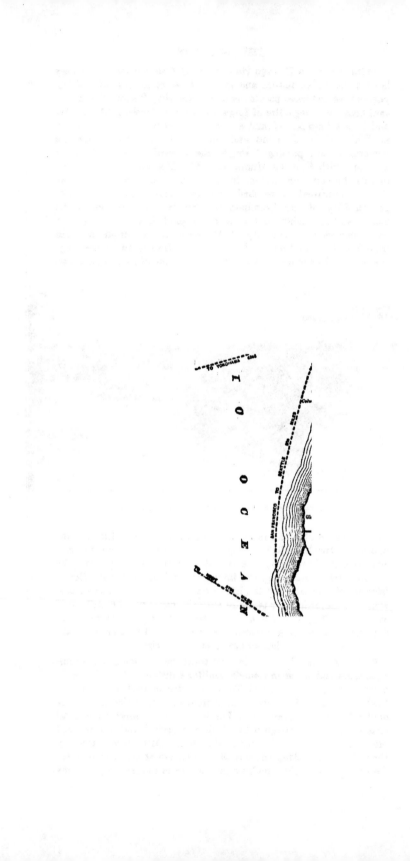

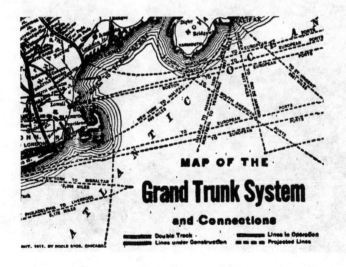

MAP OF THE

Grand Trunk System

and Connections

Double Track   Lines in Operation
Lines under Construction   Projected Lines

COPYRIGHT, 1911, BY POOLE BROS, CHICAGO.

Victoria Jubilee Bridge, across the St. Lawrence, at Montreal.

of surpassing beauty. The cities of Brantford, Woodstock and Ingersoll are passed en route before reaching London, the "Forest City" of Canada. From London the route takes the passenger through a most fertile farming district until we arrive at the great St. Clair Tunnel, "the link that binds two nations," between Sarnia, Ont., and Port Huron, Mich. This wonderful engineering feat is, with its approaches, nearly two miles long, and is one of the longest submarine tunnels in the world, costing the enormous sum of $2,700,000. This world-wonder was placed under a system of

Luncheon Hour.

electric operation at immense cost during 1908 and all passenger trains are now operated through the tunnel by powerful electric locomotives, thus doing away with all gas, dust, smoke, etc.

From Port Huron the train proceeds through the State of Michigan and parts of Indiana and Illinois, touching at Flint, Durand, Lansing and Battle Creek, Mich., and South Bend, Valparaiso and other important points in Indiana, the train arriving at Dearborn Street Station, Chicago, at 9.25 P.M., the second day out from Boston, and 24 hours from Montreal.

In addition to Tourist Sleeping Car service between Boston and Chicago, the Grand Trunk Railway System has recently placed in operation Pullman Tourist Sleeping Cars between Chicago and Buffalo. See page 19 for train schedule.

City of Toronto from Parliament Buildings.

PERSONALLY CONDUCTED EXCURSIONS WEST OF CHICAGO

Personally Conducted Excursions from Chicago after the arrival of our Personally Conducted Tourist Cars on Tuesdays, Thursdays and Saturdays, are run by various connecting lines, including the following: Via Santa Fe for California and intermediate points; Via Chicago, Milwaukee & St. Paul for points in Illinois, Iowa, Missouri, Kansas, Colorado, Utah, Nevada, California, Oregon, Washington and intermediate points; Via Chicago & Northwestern for points in Illinois, Iowa, Nebraska, Colorado, Wyoming, Utah, Nevada, California and Oregon; Via the Rock Island, to Montana; Via Chicago, Burlington & Quincy to Colorado, etc. On pages 18 and 19 of this folder are shown complete lists of various lines from Chicago west. which are subject to revision from time to time.

Kingston, Ont.

14

PULLMAN TOURIST SLEEPING CAR BERTH RATES

In addition to the cost of passage at the current second or first-class fares, there will be a small additional charge for the accommodation provided in Pullman Tourist Sleeping Cars, as follows:

BETWEEN	Boston Mass.		Montreal P.Q.		Prescott Ont.		Kingston Ont.		Toronto Ont.		Pt.Huron Mich.		Chicago Ill.	
	A	B	A	B	A	B	A	B	A	B	A	B	A	B
	$	$	$	$	$	$	$	$	$	$	$	$	$	$
St. Johns..	1.00	1.00							1.00	1.00	1.75	1.40	2.50	2.00
Montreal..	1.00	1.00											2.50	2.00
Prescott...	1.25	1.00											2.25	1.80
Kingston..	1.50	1.20											2.00	1.60
Toronto...	1.50	1.20	1.00	1.00									1.50	1.20
Hamilton..	1.75	1.40	1.00	1.00	1.00	1.00							1.50	1.20
Port Huron	2.25	1.80	1.75	1.40	1.50	1.20	1.25	1.00	1.00	1.00			1.00	1.00
Chicago....	2.75	2.20	2.50	2.00	2.25	1.80	2.00	1.60	1.50	1.20	1.00	1.00		
Buffalo....													1.50	1.20
Niagara Falls													1.50	1.20

A Lower Berth.   B Upper Berth.

The amounts named above are for a double berth, which may be occupied by two persons.

The Gorge at Winooski, Vt.

FREE RECLINING CHAIRS

Passengers for St. Paul, Winnipeg, and Western Canada, between Chicago and St. Paul, can travel in free reclining chair cars, by all routes, without extra charge. The Chicago, Burlington & Quincy Railroad also operate Tourist Sleepers between Chicago and St. Paul; cost for berth on this Coach being half the Standard Pullman Car charge. (See page 19.)

PULLMAN TOURIST SLEEPING CARS

For the accommodation of passengers holding First or Second-class Rail Tickets.

RUN THREE TIMES A WEEK BETWEEN
BOSTON, MONTREAL, ETC., AND CHICAGO

VIA BOSTON & MAINE RAILROAD, CENTRAL VERMONT RAILWAY AND
GRAND TRUNK RAILWAY SYSTEM

WESTBOUND

STATIONS	ROUTE	TIME	DAYS
(Eastern Time)			
Boston............Lv	B. & M. R.R.	11.05 AM	Mon. Wed. Fri.
Lowell............	" "	11.45 AM	" " "
Springfield........Lv	" "	12.14 PM	" " "
Providence........Lv	N. Y., N. H. & H. R.R.	7.50 AM	" " "
Worcester.........Lv	B. & M. R.R.	9.00 AM	" " "
Nashua Jct.........	" "	12.10 PM	" " "
Manchester........	" "	12.35 PM	" " "
Concord...........	" "	1.10 PM	" " "
Franklin..........	" "	1.50 PM	" " "
Enfield...........	" "	3.31 PM	" " "
Lebanon...........	" "	3.45 PM	" " "
White River Jct.....Ar	" "	3.55 PM	" " "
White River Jct.....Lv	C. V. Ry.	4.15 PM	" " "
South Royalton........	" "	4.45 PM	" " "
Bethel..........	" "	4.56 PM	" " "
Randolph..........	" "	5.13 PM	" " "
Northfield........	" "	5.56 PM	" " "
Montpelier........	" "	6.15 PM	" " "
Waterbury........Lv	" "	6.34 PM	" " "
Bellows Falls.......Lv	Rut. R.R.	3.45 PM	" " "
Rutland............	" "	4.25 PM	" " "
Burlington..........Ar	" "	6.40 PM	" " "
Burlington..........Lv	C. V. Ry	6.45 PM	" " "
Essex Jct...........	" "	7.15 PM	" " "
St. Albans.........	" "	8.00 PM	" " "
East Swanton.......	" "	8.25 PM	" " "
St. Johns.........Ar	" "	9.35 PM	" " "
St. Johns.........Lv	G. T. Ry. Sys.	9.25 PM	" " "
Montreal...........Ar	" "	10.15 PM	" " "
Portland..........Lv	G. T. Ry. Sys.	7.45 AM	" " "
Levis (Quebec)........	" "	12.30 PM	" " "
MONTREAL.......Ar	" "	6.05 PM	" " "
MONTREAL.......Lv	G. T. Ry. Sys.	10.30 PM	" " "
Cornwall.	" "	12.13 AM	Tue. Thur. Sat.
Prescott.	" "	r1.25 AM	" " "
Brockville.............	" "	1.50 AM	" " "
Kingston.............	" "	2.48 AM	" " "
Belleville.............	" "	4.25 AM	" " "
Cobourg.............	" "	5.28 AM	" " "
Port Hope Jct.........	" "	5.39 AM	" " "
Toronto............Ar	" "	7.30 AM	" " "
Toronto............Lv	" "	8.00 AM	" " "
Hamilton...........	" "	9.08 AM	" " "
Brantford..........	" "	10.00 AM	" " "
Paris..............	" "	10.13 AM	" " "
Woodstock...........	" "	10.45 AM	" " "
Ingersoll.............	" "	10.59 AM	" " "
London............	" "	11.35 AM	" " "
Strathroy.............	" "	12.06 PM	" " "
Wyoming............	" "	12.38 PM	" " "
Sarnia Tunnel.......Ar	" "	1.02 PM	" " "
(Central Time)			
Port Huron........Lv	" "	12.40 PM	" " "
Flint..............	" "	2.10 PM	" " "
Durand.............	" "	2.36 PM	" " "
Lansing............	" "	3.36 PM	" " "
Battle Creek...........	" "	4.35 PM	" " "
South Bend...........	" "	6.42 PM	" " "
CHICAGO.........Ar	" "	9.35 PM	" " "

Passengers from Springfield join car at White River Junction or Montreal; from Providence and Worcester at Nashua Junction; from Montpelier at Montpelier Junction; from Bellows Falls, Rutland and Burlington at Essex Junction, and from Portland, Me., Levis (Quebec), Halifax, N.S., or St. John, N.B., at Montreal.

r Will stop to let off passengers from Montreal or beyond and to pick up passengers for Toronto or beyond.

PULLMAN TOURIST SLEEPING CARS

For the accommodation of passengers holding First or Second-class Rail Tickets.

RUN THREE TIMES A WEEK BETWEEN
CHICAGO, MONTREAL AND BOSTON
VIA GRAND TRUNK RAILWAY SYSTEM, CENTRAL VERMONT RAILWAY
AND BOSTON & MAINE RAILROAD

EASTBOUND

STATIONS	ROUTE	TIME	DAYS
(Central Time)			
CHICAGO.........Lv	G. T. Ry. Sys.	3.30 PM	Wed. Thur. Sat.
South Bend............	" "	6.72 PM	" " "
Battle Creek...........	" "	8.34 PM	" " "
Lansing...............	" "	9.44 PM	" " "
Durand...............	" "	10.37 PM	" " "
Flint.................	" "	11.10 PM	" " "
Port Huron..........Ar	" "	12.50 AM	Thur. Fri. Sun.
(Eastern Time)			
Sarnia Tunnel.,.....Lv	" "	2.15 AM	" " "
Strathroy...............	" "	f 3.11 AM	" " "
London..............	" "	3.48 AM	" " "
Ingersoll	" "	4.16 AM	" " "
Woodstock	" "	4.33 AM	" " "
Paris..............	" "	d5.00 AM	" " "
Brantford............	" "	5 15 AM	" " "
Hamilton	" "	7 00 AM	" " "
Toronto............Ar	" "	8.25 AM	" " "
Toronto............Lv	" "	9.00 AM	" " "
Port Hope Jct......Ar..	" "	10.49 AM	" " "
Cobourg.............	" "	11.01 AM	" " "
Belleville.....}	" "	12.11 PM	" " "
Napanee.............	" "	12.46 PM	" " "
Kingston............	" "	1.40 PM	" " "
Gananoque Jct.......	" "	1.50 PM	" " "
Brockville...........	" "	2.40 PM	" " "
Prescott.............	" "	3.03 PM	" " "
Cornwall............	" "	4.10 PM	" " "
MONTREAL........Ar	" "	6.00 PM	" " "
MONTREAL......Lv	G. T. Ry. Sys.	8.15 PM	" " "
Levis (Qu ec) ......Ar	" "	7.40 AM	Fri. Sat. Mon.
Portland............Ar	" "	7.30 AM	" " "
MONTREAL.......Lv	G. T. Ry. Sys.	8.30 PM	Thurs. Fri. Sun.
St. Johns..........Ar	" "	9.20 PM	" " "
St. Johns..........Lv	C. V. Ry.	9.25 PM	" " "
East Swanton........	" "	10.26 PM	" " "
St. Albans............	" "	10.55 PM	" " "
Essex Jct............	" "	11.42 PM	" " "
Burlington ....Ar	" "	12.05 AM	Fri. Sat. Mon.
Burlington Lv	Rut. R.R.	8.15 AM	" " "
Rutland.............Ar	" "	10.50 AM	" " "
Bellows Falls........Ar	" "	1.05 PM	" " "
Waterbury..........Ar	C. V. Ry.	12.24 AM	" " "
Montpelier...........	" "	12.52 AM	" " "
Northfield...........	" "	1.20 AM	" " "
Randolph............	" "	2.15 AM	" " "
Bethel..............	" "	2.28 AM	" " "
South Royalton.......	" "	2.42 AM	" " "
White River Jct......Ar	" "	3.20 AM	" " "
White River Jct......Lv	B. & M. R.R.	3.40 AM	" " "
Lebanon.............	" "	3.54 AM	" " "
Enfield..............	" "	4.09 AM	" " "
Franklin.............	" "	5.21 AM	" " "
Concord.............	" "	5.54 AM	" " "
Manchester..........	" "	6.27 AM	" " "
Nashua Jct..........	" "	6.55 AM	" " "
Worcester...........Ar	" "	9.14 AM	" " "
Providence..........Ar	N. Y., N. H. & H. R.R.	12.00 PM	" " "
Springfield..........Ar	B. & M. R.R.	7.35 AM	" " "
Lowell..............	" "	7.19 AM	" " "
Boston.............Ar	" "	8.05 AM	" " "

Passengers for Portland, Me., Quebec, Halifax, N.S., or St. John, N.B. will leave car at Montreal; for Burlington, Rutland and Bellows Falls at Essex Junction; for Montpelier at Montpelier Junction; for Worcester and Providence at Nashua Junction, and for Springfield, Mass., at Montreal or White River Junction.

d Will stop to let off passengers from points beyond Port Huron.

17

TOURIST SLEEPING CAR SERVICE FROM CHICAGO TO THE WEST

WESTBOUND	Berth Rate from Chicago	Via A. T. & S. F. Ry., Daily	Via C. B. & Q., D. & R. G., S. P. L. A. & S. L. Route, Daily	Via A. T. & S. F. Ry., Daily	Via C. & N. W., Nor. Pac. Daily	Via C. & N. W., U. P., O. S. L. and Salt Lake Route, Daily	Via C. & N. W., U. P., O. R. L., Ore.-Wash. R. & N. Co., Va Granger, Daily	Via C. & N. W., U. P., So. Pac. Daily	Via C. & N. W., U. P., So. ¼ ac. Daily	Via Rock Island Lines, El Paso & S. W. Rys., So. Pac. Daily	Via Rock Island Lines, D. & R. G., Sou. Pacific. Thur., Fri.	Via Rock Island Lines, D. & R. G. Western Pac. Sun. Mon. Wed., Sat.
Chicago ... Lv	$1.25	1st day, 9 30	1st day, 11 00	1st day, 10 00	1st day, 10 00	1st day, 10 00	1st day, 8 30	1st day, 10 45	1st day, 8 30	1st day, 8 35	1st day,	1st day, 10 30
Kansas City ... Ar	1.25	1st day, 8 15	2d day, 3 55	2d day, 11 00			2d day, 9 15	2d day, 9 15	2d day, 9 15	1st day, 11 00	2d day,	2d day, 1 40
Omaha ... Ar	4.25											
Albuquerque ... Lv	8.00	3d day, 12 45	3d day,	3d day, 8 10		2d day, 11 40					3d day, 9 00	3d day, 8 00
Denver ... Lv	6.00		3d day, 7 20								3d day, 11 45	3d day, 10 3.
Colorado Springs ... Lv	6.00		3d day, 11 45								3d day, 1 30	3d day, 11 50
Pueblo ... Lv	6.00		3d day, 1 20								3d day, 2 00	3d day,
Ogden ... Ar	4.75		4th day, 2 25		4th day, 7 45	3d day, 3 35	4th day, 8 30		3d day, 6 15	3d day, 1 25	3d day, 6 50	4th day,
Salt Lake City ... Ar	7.00				4th day, 8 15	3d day, 4 45	4th day, 4 40		3d day, 7 55	3d day, 5 40	3d day, 8 15	4th day, 12 35
Portland ... Ar					4th day, 8 15		4th day, 6 15					
Tacoma ... Ar												
Seattle ... Ar	4.50	3d day, 6 20	5th day,	5th day, 5 30		4th day, 4 30	5th day, 6 30		4th day, 1 20	3d day,		5th day, 6 30
El Paso ... Ar	7.00	4th day, 6 20	5th day, 3 30	5th day, 8 30					5th day, 9 45		6th day, 12 00	
San Francisco ... Ar	7.00	4th day, 6 15	5th day, 8 30	5th day, 1 10		4th day, 8 30	5th day, 8 40		5th day, 1 10		6th day, 7 15	8th day,
Los Angeles ... Ar	7.00	4th day, 1 10	6th day, 7 00	6th day, 1 10		4th day, 4 40	5th day, 6 15		5th day, 1 30			
San Diego (a) ... Ar												8th day, 6 30

WESTBOUND	Berth Rate from Chicago	Via C. B. & Q., D. & R. G. and Western Pacific Tu., Thur., Fri.	Via C. B. & Q. and Gt. Northern. Daily	Via C. B. & Q., D. & R. G. and So. Pac. Mon., Wed. and Sat.	Via C. B. & Q. and No. Pac. Daily	Via C. M. & St. P., C. M. & St. P. Daily	Via C. M. & St. P., U. P., So. Pac. Daily	Via C. M. & St. P., O. R. & N. Wash., Ore., R. & N. Co. Daily	Via (C. M. & St. P., U. P., O. S. L. and Salt Lake Route Daily	Via C. M. & St. P., U. P., O. S. L., Salt Lake Route. 2d day.	Via I., So. Pac. to New Orleans. Monday
Chicago ... Lv	$1.25	1st day, 11 00	1st day, 10 15	1st day, 11 00	1st day, 9 30	1st day, 10 10	1st day, 10 15	1st day, 9 00	1st day, 10 00	1st day, 10 45	1st day, 9 10
Kansas City ... Ar	1.25	2d day, 3 45		2d day, 3 35				2d day,	1st day, 11 45	2d day, 12 35	
Omaha ... Ar	4.25										
Albuquerque ... Lv	8.00	3d day, 7 20		3d day, 7 20							
Denver ... Lv	6.00	3d day, 11 45		3d day, 11 45							
Colorado Springs ... Lv	6.00	3d day, 1 20		3d day, 1 20						3d day, 6 50	
Pueblo ... Lv	6.00									3d day, 8 15	
Ogden ... Ar	4.75	4th day, 2 25	4th day, 7 45	4th day, 2 25	4th day, 8 10	4th day, 12 35	3d day,	3d day, 6 15			
Salt Lake City ... Ar	7.00		4th day, 10 00		4th day, 11 15	4th day, 11 10	3d day, 7 55	4th day, 11 40			
Portland ... Ar			4th day, 8 15		4th day, 11 0.			4th day, 7 00			
Tacoma ... Ar								4th day, 8 30			
Seattle ... Ar	4.50	5th day, 8 30		5th day, 8 30						4th day, 6 50	
El Paso ... Ar	7.00									5th day, 9 15	
San Francisco ... Ar	7.00	6th day, 4 30		6th day, 2 45		6th day, 1 20				5th day, 10 30	
Los Angeles ... Ar	7.00					8th day,		6th day, (b) 8 45			

(a) Times shown to San Diego are the times at which passengers should arrive there, but with the exception of the A. T. & S. F. route tourist cars do not run beyond Los Angeles.

(b) Monday, Wednesday and Friday to Los Angeles. A.M. times shown in light-face figures thus, 6 00; P.M. times in bold-face figures thus, **6 00.**

18

PULLMAN TOURIST SLEEPING CARS
BETWEEN CHICAGO, LONDON, HAMILTON AND BUFFALO
VIA GRAND TRUNK RAILWAY SYSTEM AND LEHIGH VALLEY R.R.

EASTBOUND				WESTBOUND		
STATION	Route	Exp. Daily		STATION	Route	Exp. Daily
		P.M.				P.M.
CHICAGO.........(C.T.) Lv	G.T.R.Sys	*3 30		BUFFALO...(E.T.) Lv	L.V.R.R.	*12 50
Port Huron..............Lv	"	1 00		Niagara Falls, N.Y..Lv	"	
Suspension Bridge(E.T.)Ar	"	7 30		Suspension Bridge Lv	G.T.R.Sys	
Niagara Falls, N.Y.......Ar	L.V.R.R.	7 47		Port Huron..(C.T.) Ar	"	
BUFFALO ....Ar	"	*8 52		CHICAGO...........Ar	"	*8 00
		A.M.				A.M.

TOURIST SLEEPING CAR SERVICE
FROM CHICAGO TO NORTH PACIFIC POINTS VIA ST. PAUL

WESTBOUND	Berth Rates from Chicago	Via C. B. & Q. and Gt. Nor. Rys. Daily		Via C. B. & Q. and Nor. Pac. Rys. Daily	
Chicago.................Lv	.....	1st day,	10 15	1st day,	9 30
St. Paul................Lv	$1.00	2d day,	11 15	1st day,	10 30
Minneapolis.............Lv	1.00	2d day,	11 45	1st day,	11 00
Spokane.................Ar	5.75	4th day,	6 30	3d day,	9 20
Seattle.................Ar	6.75	4th day,	8 15	4th day,	11 00
Tacoma.................Ar	6.75	4th day,	10 10	4th day,	11 15
Portland................Ar	6.75	4th day,	7 40	4th day,	8 10

TABLE OF CONNECTIONS FROM CHICAGO TO MEXICO

STATIONS	Via C. & E. I. Frisco, G. C. & S. F., Int. & G. N. Nat. Lines of Mexico		I. C., S. P. and National Lines of Mexico. Via New Orleans		Wabash, Iron Mountain, Tex. & Pacific, Int. & G. N. and N. L. of M.		C. & A., St. L., I.M. & S., T. & P., I. & G. N. and Nat. Lines of Mexico	
Chicago Lv	1st day,	9 20	1st day,	9 10	1st day,	12 02	1st day,	11 30
St. Louis...........Lv	1st day,	7 57			1st day,	8 51	1st day,	8 51
Texarkana.......Ar					2d day,	12 20	2d day,	12 20
New Orleans....Ar	2d day,	5 20	2d day,	10 55				
Paris..............Ar	2d day,	5 20						
San Antonio......Ar	3d day,	9 55	3d day,	7 30	3d day,	6 35	3d day,	6 35
Laredo............Ar	4th day,	12 55			3d day,	12 55	3d day,	12 55
Monterey.........Ar	4th day,	6 50			3d day,	6 50	3d day,	6 50
Saltillo ....Ar	4th day,	10 40			3d day,	10 25	3d day,	10 25
S n Luis Potosi .Ar	5th day,	7 05			4th day,	7 05	4th day,	7 05
Gonzales ....Ar	5th day,	12 25			4th day,	12 25	4th day,	12 25
Queretaro........Ar	5th day,	1 30	5th day,	1 30	4th day,	1 30	4th day,	1 30
Mexico.... ......Ar	5th day,	8 00	5th day,	8 00	4th day,	8 00	4th day,	8 00

A.M. times shown in light-face figures. P.M. times in full-face figures.

LIST OF PUBLICATIONS

Copies of any of the following will be furnished free upon application to any of the Passenger and Traveling Agents appearing on page 30 of this folder

GRAND TRUNK RAILWAY SYSTEM

"Muskoka Lakes—Highlands of Ontario." "Lake of Bays—Highlands of Ontario." "Among the 30,000 Islands of Georgian Bay." "Trains Three and Four." "Across Niagara's Gorge," "Ste Anne de Bellevue," "Orillia and Couchiching," "Mount Clemens," "Haunts of Fish and Game," "Timagami," "Algonquin National Park," "Montreal Quebec and Ottawa," "Porcupine and Cobalt," "Vistas," "Playgrounds of Canada," "Mountains of New England and the Sea," "Lake Resorts, Michigan and Indiana," "Tourist Sleeping Cars." "International Limited."

PASSENGER AND TRAVELING AGENTS

ALEXANDRIA BAY, N.Y.Cornwall Bros.....Ticket Agents, Market St.
BATTLE CREEK, MICH. L. J. Bush.........Passenger Agent, G. T. Ry. Station.
BAY CITY, MICH........Geo. W. Watson....Passenger Agent, G. T. Ry. Station.
BOSTON, MASS..........E. H. Boynton.....New Eng. Pass'r Agt., 256 Washington St.
    "   "   .....J. M. Shea........Traveling Pass'r Agt., 256 Washington St.
BROCKVILLE, ONT.....J. H. Fulford......Ticket Agent, 8 Court House Ave.
BUFFALO, N.Y.........H. M. Morgan......City Pass'r and Ticket Agt., 285 Main St.
    (Elliott Sq. Building).
BURLINGTON, VT.......M. S. Rooney......Traveling Passenger Agt., 170 College St.
    "   ....H. H. Hickok......City Passenger Agt., 170 College St.
CHICAGO, ILL.........C. G. Orttenburger, City Pass'r and Ticket Agt., 301 South
    Clark St., cor. Jackson Boulevard.
    "   "   .....Franks Ticket and Tourist Co., 121 South Clark St.
    "   "   .....F. E. Scott......Tkt. Agt. Auditorium Annex, Mich. Av.
    and Congress St. and Palmer House.
    "   "   .....O. C. Bryant......Trav. Pass'r Agt., Room 917, Merchants'
    Loan and Trust Building.
    "   "   .....Gay W. Norman, L. C. Russell, C. W. Bell, T.P. Agts., Room
    917, Merchants' Loan and Trust Building.
DETROIT, MICH........Fred C. Wherrett..Trav. Pass'r Agt., 118 Woodward Ave.
    "   ....C. M. Harwood.....C. P. & T. A., 118 Woodward Ave.
FLINT, MICH..........V. A. Bovee.......Passenger Agent, G. T. Ry. Station.
FORT WILLIAM, ONT....Ray Street & Co...Ticket Agents, 201-305 Simpson St.
GRAND RAPIDS, MICH...C. A. Justin......City Passenger and Ticket Agt., Morton
    House Block, 78 Monroe Avenue.
HAMILTON, ONT........C. R. Morgan......City Pass'r and Tkt. Agt., 11 James St.. N.
HOLYOKE, MASS........A. Therrien.......Traveling Passenger Agent, 50 West St.
KANSAS CITY, MO......W. M. Lewis.......Trav. Pass'r Agent, 827 Sheidley Bldg.
KINGSTON, ONT........P. Hanley.........City Pass'r and Ticket Agent, 67 Earl St.
LANSING, MICH........F. H. Potter......Passenger Agent, G. T. Ry. Station.
LEWISTON, ME.........F. P. Chandler....Passenger Agent, G. T. Ry. Station.
LONDON, ONT..........R. E. Ruse........City Passenger and Ticket Agent, cor.
    Richmond and Dundas Sts.
LOS ANGELES, CAL.....W. H. Bullen......Pacific Coast Agent, 302 Wilcox Bldg.
MILWAUKEE, WIS.......Crosby Trans. Co. 308 East Water Street.
MONCTON, N.B.........J. H. Corcoran....Traveling Pass'r Agt., 8 Wise Building
    Main Street.
MONTREAL, QUE........J. Quinlan........Dist. Pass'r Agt., Bonaventure Station.
    "   "   ....R. McC. Smith....Special Passenger Agent.
    "   "   .......M.O. Dafoe, W. S. Miller, J. E. Crossley, Traveling Pas-
    senger Agts., Bonaventure Sta.
    "   "   ....W. H. Clanc......City Pass'r and Tkt. Agt., 122 St. James St.
    cor. St. Francois Xavier
    "   "   ....W. H. O'Donnell..Steamship Agent, 122 St. James St., cor.
    St. Francois Xavier.
MT. CLEMENS, MICH....Casper Czizek....City Pass'r and T. Agt., 12 N- Gratiot Ave.
NEW LONDON, CONN.....M. M. Driscoll....Traveling Passenger Agent.
NEW YORK, N.Y........F. P. Dwyer.......Gen. Agent, Passenger Dept., Railway
    Exchange, 290 Broadway.
NIAGARA FALLS, N.Y...D. Isaacs.........Ticket Agent, Prospect House.
    "   "   ...W. R. Prescott...City Pass'r and Ticket Agt., 1 Falls St.
NIAGARA FALLS, ONT...G. R. Major.......Ticket Agent, Clifton Hotel.
OGDENSBURG, N.Y......Geo. S. Meagher..Ticket Agent, 55 State Street.
OTTAWA, ONT..........Percy M. Buttler,.City Pass'r and Ticket Agent, Russell
    House Blk. cor. Sparks and Elgin Sts.
PETERBORO, ONT.......R. A. Rose........City Pass'r and Tkt. Agt., 334 George St.
PITTSBURG, PA........A. B. Chown......Trav. Passenger Agt., 507 Park Building.
PORT HURON, MICH.....T. C. Mann........Ticket Agent, G.T.Ry. Station.
    "   .....E. F. Percival....City Pass'r and Tkt. Agt., 1002 Military St.
PORTLAND, ME.........C. E. Tenny......Passenger Agent, G. T. Ry. Station.
PORTLAND, ORE........Dorsey B. Smith..City Pass. Agent, 80 Fifth Ave., Com-
    mercial Club Building.
PRINCE RUPERT, B.C...A. Davidson......General Agent, Centre Street.
QUEBEC, QUE..........Geo. H. Stott....C. P. & T. A., cor. St. Anne and DuFort
    Sts. and Ferry Ldg., Dalhousie St.
SAGINAW, MICH........Hugh E. Quick....Passenger Agent, G. T. Ry. Station.
SAN FRANCISCO, CAL...F. W. Hopper.....Gen. Agent, Passenger Dept., 809 Monad-
    nock Building.
SEATTLE, WASH........J. H. Burgis.....Gen. Agent, Passenger Dept., First Ave.
    and Yesler Way.
    "   "   ....J. H. Goodier....City Passenger and Ticket Agent, First
    Ave. and Yesler Way.
SHERBROOKE, QUE......C. H. Foss........City Pass'r and Tkt. Agt., 2 Wellington St.
SOUTH BEND, IND......C. A. McNutt.....Passenger Agent, G. T. Ry. Station.
SPRINGFIELD, MASS....A. C. Wentworth..City Passenger Agent, 12 East Court St.
ST. PAUL, MINN.......W. J. Gilkerson..G. A. P. D., 40 Robert St.
TORONTO, ONT.........C. E. Horning....District Passenger Agent, Union Station.
    "   "   ....C. S. Proctor....Traveling Pass'r Agent, Union Station.
    "   "   ....W. J. Moffat, Jas. Anderson, Trav. Pass'r Agts., Union Sta.
    "   "   ....C. E. Jenney.....City Passenger and Ticket Agent, North-
    west corner King and Yonge Sts.
VANCOUVER, B.C.......W. E. Duperow....Gen. Agt. Pass'r Dept., 527 Granville St.
    "   "   ....H. G. Smith......City Pass'r and Tkt. Agt., 527 Granville
    St. and G.T.P. Dock foot of Main St.
VICTORIA, B.C........C. F. Earle.......City Pass'r and Tkt. Agt. G. T. P. Dock.
WINNIPEG, MAN........W. J. Quinlan....District Passenger Agt., 260 Portage Ave.
    "   "   ....H. J. Lambkin....Traveling Pass'r Agent, 260 Portage Ave.
WORCESTER, MASS......C. E. Belanger....Trav. Passenger Agt., 10 Lamartine St.
    "   ....Geo. O. Le Vassuer, Passenger Agt., 28 Washington Sq.

EUROPEAN TRAFFIC DEPARTMENT

F. C. Salter, European Traffic Mgr., 17-19 Cockspur St., London. S.W., England.
AMSTERDAM and THE HAGUE HOLLAND, Messrs. Hoyman and Schuurman, Gen.
    Pass. and Tourist Office.
ANTWERP, BELGIUM....P. A. Clews, Acting Gen. Agt., 19-21 Canal des Brasseurs.
BIRMINGHAM, ENG.....Morison, Pollexfen & Blair, No. 6 Victoria Square.
GLASGOW, SCOTLAND...J. M. Walker......General Agent, 5 Union Street.
LIVERPOOL ENG.......Wm. Cuthbertson,.General Assistant, 30 Water St.
LONDON, S.W., ENG...F. G. English.....Gen. Agt., Frt. Dept., 17-19 Cockspur St.
LONDON, S.W. ENG....J. Herson.........Pass'r Agt., 17-19 Cockspur St.
LONDON, E.C. ENG....P. A. Clews.......City Agent, 44-45-46 Leadenhall St.
PARIS, FRANCE.......Pitt & Scott.....Ticket Agents, 47 Rue Cambon
SHEFFIELD, ENG......J. W. Dawson .....Agent, No. 7 Haymarket.

G. T. BELL.
Passenger Traffic Manager,
MONTREAL.

H. G. ELLIOTT.
General Passenger Agent,
MONTREAL.

Winooski River near Middlesex, Vt.

GRAND TRUNK RAILWAY SYSTEM'S EUROPEAN ORGANIZATION

The Grand Trunk System has a most complete organisation in Europe, with every facility at their disposal to help passengers to reach their points of destination in Canada and United States, and at their different offices a list of which can be found in this publication, ocean and rail tickets are issued and arrangements can be made for forwarding baggage and covering same with insurance. They are also in a position to supply travellers with convenient forms for carrying money, viz.: Canadian Express Money Orders, which may be cashed anywhere in dollars and cents. It will be to the advantage of travellers to consult with any of the European Agencies, where the latest publication dealing with Canada can be secured free.

Trans-Atlantic passengers visiting London, Eng., are cordially invited to visit the handsomely equipped new offices of the Grand Trunk System at 17-19 Cockspur Street, London, S. W., Eng. The site of this new building is one of the best in the great Metropolitan City, and in the midst of the busiest centre of London; in fact it is at the very hub of the world's metropolis. It is within five minutes' walk of a half dozen of the leading hotels, and adjacent to Trafalgar Square, Bakerloo and Picadilly Tubes. Motor buses pass the door every few seconds to all parts of London — North, South, East and West.

Reception rooms have been sumptuously furnished for the use and comfort of visitors, where writing material may be found and the leading daily newspapers of Canada are on file.

The Grand Trunk are in a position to book passage to Canada and the United States via any of the ocean routes. This is a great convenience to tourists and business men visiting England or the continent.

Courteous representatives of the Company are in attendance to give all information to enquirers, and to see that visitors are made at home. If desired, correspondence may be addressed in care of this office.

Offices, London, Eng.
Grand Trunk System—Canadian Express Co.

22

CPSIA information can be obtained
at www.ICGtesting.com
Printed in the USA
BVHW090054211118
533618BV00024B/3518/P